FRANCIS FRITH'S
AROUND
PLYMOUTH
PHOTOGRAPHIC MEMORIES

MARTIN DUNNING spent several years teaching before escaping the classroom to pursue a career as a freelance writer. He has written for 'The Western Morning News' and the climbing magazine 'High', and is the author of several walking, travel and local history books. Martin has lived in Devon for 40 years.

BEDFORD STREET *1904* 52407

FRANCIS FRITH'S

AROUND

PLYMOUTH

PHOTOGRAPHIC MEMORIES

MARTIN DUNNING

First published in the United Kingdom in 2000 by
The Francis Frith Collection

Hardback edition 2000
ISBN 1-85937-119-1

Reprinted in hardback 2001

Paperback edition 2001
ISBN 1-85937-389-5

Reprinted in paperback 2003, 2004

Revised and extended paperback edition published in 2006
ISBN 1-84589-366-2

British Library Cataloguing in Publication Data

Around Plymouth Photographic Memories
Martin Dunning

The Francis Frith Collection®
Frith's Barn, Teffont,
Salisbury, Wiltshire SP3 5QP
Tel: +44 (0) 1722 716 376
Email: info@francisfrith.co.uk
www.francisfrith.com

Aerial photographs reproduced under licence from Simmons Aerofilms Limited
Historical Ordnance Survey maps reproduced under licence from Homecheck.co.uk

Printed and bound in England

Front Cover: **PLYMOUTH,** The Barbican 1890 22474t

The colour-tinting in this image is for illustrative purposes only,
and is not intended to be historically accurate

CONTENTS

THE MAKING OF AN ARCHIVE

FRANCIS FRITH, Victorian founder of the world-famous photographic archive, was a devout Quaker and a highly successful Victorian businessman. By 1860 he was already a multi-millionaire, having established and sold a wholesale grocery business in Liverpool. He had also made a series of pioneering photographic journeys to the Nile region. The images he returned with were the talk of London. An eminent modern historian has likened their impact on the population of the time to that on our own generation of the first photographs taken on the surface of the moon.

Frith had a passion for landscape, and was as equally inspired by the countryside of Britain as he was by the desert regions of the Nile. He resolved to set out on a new career and to use his skills with a camera. He established a business in Reigate as a specialist publisher of topographical photographs.

Frith lived in an era of immense and sometimes violent change. For the poor in the early part of Victoria's reign work was a drudge and the hours long, and ordinary people had precious little free time. Most had not travelled far beyond the boundaries of their own town or village. Mass tourism was in its infancy during the 1860s, but during the next decade the railway network and the establishment of Bank Holidays and half-Saturdays gradually made it possible for the working man and his family to enjoy holidays and to see a little more of the world. With characteristic business acumen, Francis Frith foresaw that these new tourists would enjoy having souvenirs to commemorate their days out. He began selling photo-souvenirs of seaside resorts and beauty spots, which the Victorian public pasted into treasured family albums.

Frith's aim was to photograph every town and village in Britain. For the next thirty years he travelled the country by train and by pony and trap, producing fine photographs of seaside resorts and beauty spots that were keenly bought by millions of Victorians.

THE RISE OF FRITH & CO

Each photograph was taken with tourism in mind, the small team of Frith photographers concentrating on busy shopping streets, beaches, seafronts, picturesque lanes and villages. They also photographed buildings: the Victorian and Edwardian eras were times of huge building activity, and town halls, libraries, post offices, schools and technical colleges were springing up all over the country. They were invariably celebrated by a proud Victorian public, and photo souvenirs – visual records – published by F Frith & Co were sold in their hundreds of thousands. In addition, many new commercial buildings such as hotels, inns and pubs were photographed, often because their owners specifically commissioned Frith postcards or prints of them for re-sale or for publicity purposes.

In order to gain some understanding of the scale of Frith's business one only has to look at the catalogue issued by Frith & Co in 1886: it runs to some 670 pages. By 1890 Frith had created the greatest specialist photographic publishing company in the world, with over 2,000 stockists! The picture on the right shows the Frith & Co display board on the wall of the stockist at Ingleton in the Yorkshire Dales (left of window). Beautifully constructed with a mahogany frame and gilt inserts, it displayed a dozen scenes.

POSTCARD BONANZA

The ever-popular holiday postcard we know today took many years to appear, and F Frith & Co was in the vanguard of its development. Postcards became a hugely popular means of communication and sold in their millions. Frith's company took full advantage of this boom and soon became the major publisher of photographic view postcards.

Francis Frith died in 1898 at his villa in Cannes, his great project still growing. His sons Eustace and Cyril continued their father's monumental task, expanding the number of views offered to the public and recording more and more places in Britain, as the coasts and countryside were opened up to mass travel. The archive Frith created

continued in business for another seventy years. By 1970 it contained over a third of a million pictures of 7,000 cities, towns and villages. The massive photographic record Frith has left to us stands as a living monument to a special and very remarkable man.

This book shows Plymouth as it was photographed by this world-famous archive at various periods in its development over the past 150 years. Every photograph was taken for a specific commercial purpose, which explains why the selection may not show every aspect of the town landscape. However, the photographs, compiled from one of the world's most celebrated archives, provide an important and absorbing record of the city.

INTRODUCTION

DESPITE the role it has played in many of Britain's great historic moments and periods, Plymouth is a city apart. Although only 200 miles from London - the same distance as, say, Manchester or Liverpool - its location on the far south-west peninsula has given Plymouth an isolation, even today, that other great cities lack. And it is not merely distance that has isolated the city - its site is bounded on all sides by obstacles. To the north are the stern hills of Dartmoor, to the east the River Plym and to the west the Tamar. Early visitors to the peninsula on which the city would eventually grow would have had to wait for the tide at the Ebb Ford, where Marsh Mills roundabout now stands, before they could cross the Plym and put their feet up at the Crabtree Inn, which over the centuries welcomed many a tired and mud-spattered traveller. Those coming from the west had two choices: to travel north to Gunnislake, the lowest bridge on the Tamar and some twenty miles up the river, and thence via Tavistock and Roborough Down, or to take the ferry that ran at Saltash across the strong tides of the Tamar. Even for land travellers, Plymouth was a place governed by the tides.

Plymouth grew from several small settlements, one of the earliest being Mountbatten, at the mouth of the Plym.

The site of an Iron Age cemetery, Mountbatten is thought to have been a trading post from as early as 1000 BC, and in Roman times exported cattle, hides and tin - the first indication of the maritime future of the area. Opposite Mountbatten the small fishing village of Sutton grew around the sheltered harbour of Sutton Pool; it eventually became a town when it was granted a market in 1254 by Henry III. By this time, ships loading tin from the rich port of Plympton had started to use Sutton too, and a lively trade was developing. Fish, hides, lead, wool and cloth were exported, while iron, fruit, wine, onions, garlic and wheat were landed.

1295 saw an event that was to point the way for future development when Edward I assembled the fleet at Plymouth for the first time. The port occupies a crucial strategic position guarding the Western Approaches; it was this factor that was to cement Plymouth's importance, and was probably a consideration when Henry VI granted the borough charter in 1439.

If Plymouth's maritime status brought prosperity, it also meant that the port was often in the front line, especially when Spain was involved. Francis Drake, knighted by Elizabeth I for his circumnavigation of the globe in 1577-80, sailed from Plymouth to 'singe the King of Spain's

Right: **BEDFORD STREET** *1913* 65976

Opposite: **DRAKE'S ISLAND** *1890* 22426

beard' at Cadiz in 1587 and returned to face his sternest test in 1588 - the Spanish Armada. His apparent bravado on insisting that he finish his game of bowls before engaging the mighty Spanish fleet was dictated by the mundane fact that his ships could not sail until the tide had turned, but what is not in doubt is that his courage and seamanship helped carry the day for the English fleet. Drake did not, as is commonly believed, command the fleet - that responsibility fell to Lord Howard.

Years of fighting Catholic Spain probably explain the streak of puritanism that Plymouth showed for the next hundred years. The city welcomed the noncomformist Pilgrim Fathers when the Mayflower put in for repairs and provisions before sailing for the New World in 1620, and during the Civil War it took Cromwell's side. Plymouth was isolated, as Barnstaple, Bideford and Exeter were all captured by the Royalists and Royalist ships blockaded the Sound.

The nine thousand Parliamentarian troops garrisoned at Plymouth held out under siege for two years, winning a famous victory in December 1643 in the battle which raged around Tothill and Freedom Park. Prince Maurice Road and Mount Gould are named after the Royalist and Parliamentarian commanders. Plymouth was eventually relieved in March 1645 when Cromwell and Fairfax met in the city.

Upon the Restoration of the Monarchy, Charles II decided that Plymouth's defences needed strengthening and commissioned the building of the Citadel. One of the finest and largest restoration forts in the country, it boasted upon completion 152 guns, some of which faced the city as a reminder to Plymothians of their true place in the order of things.

Secretary of the Navy Samuel Pepys, now known for his diaries but also effectively the founder of the Royal Navy as we know it, visited Plymouth with Charles

INTRODUCTION

in 1676 to inspect sites for a new Royal Dockyard. Turnchapel, at the mouth of the Plym, was considered, but eventually the prize was given to the Tamar. The Tamar's disadvantages - strong tides, a narrow and winding entrance and often contrary winds - also acted in its favour as they gave the river natural defences from attack; work started on what is now Devonport's South Yard in 1691. Another sign of the port's growing stature was the building in 1696 of Winstanley's 120-foot lighthouse on the Eddystone Rocks fourteen miles off the Hoe, the first in a series of four that would culminate in the current lighthouse built by Douglas in 1878.

Investment notwithstanding, Plymouth struggled for the first half of the 18th century. Fishing still thrived, particularly for pilchards, and trade carried on, but Plymouth has never figured near the top of the table as a commercial port because of its isolation and the lack of nearby markets. Bristol and Liverpool made fortunes from the slave trade, and London's demand for commodities ensured that her docks were always busy, but Plymouth slumbered on, depressed and waiting for a turn in the tides of history.

War, by now a recurring theme in the fortunes of the city, provided the catalyst. From 1756 a succession of conflicts - the Seven Years' War, the American War of Independence and the Napoleonic Wars - caused an upturn in Plymouth's fortunes. Her isolation was eased in 1758 with the completion of the Great West Road, although it still took twelve hours to reach Exeter. The Royal Naval Hospital in Stonehouse was built in 1758-62, the dockyard bustled, and in 1812 the famous Scots engineer John Rennie began the construction of the Breakwater. A massive undertaking which was not completed until 1841, the Breakwater was a crucial development. Generations of mariners such as Grenville, Howard and Raleigh had complained that the relatively narrow entrances to the Plym and Tamar were dangerous

in foul weather; mariners would often run before the storm to anchor in the sheltered waters of Tor Bay. Now, all a gale-battered ship had to do was slip in through the eastern or western entrances and move into the lee of the breakwater, with plenty of sea-room and calm water in which to anchor.

The railways arrived in 1848-9, and at last Plymouth had a rapid connection with the rest of the country. Isambard Kingdom Brunel's magnificent railway bridge over the Tamar, completed shortly before the great man's death in 1859, had more than a mere practical significance - it was a symbol of Plymouth moving with the times.

John Foulston's Theatre Royal provided entertainment for those who could afford it, while those of lesser means could promenade on the pier or take the air on the Hoe. In the 1920s and 1930s, transatlantic liners anchored in the Sound, discharging passengers such as Charlie Chaplin, Mary Pickford and Rudolph Valentino to catch their train for London from Millbay Docks.

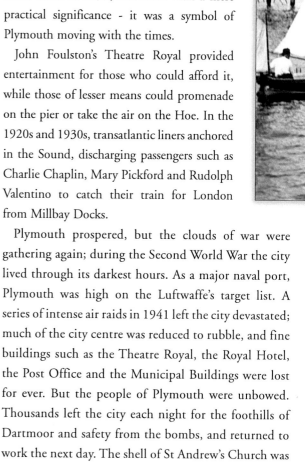

Plymouth prospered, but the clouds of war were gathering again; during the Second World War the city lived through its darkest hours. As a major naval port, Plymouth was high on the Luftwaffe's target list. A series of intense air raids in 1941 left the city devastated; much of the city centre was reduced to rubble, and fine buildings such as the Theatre Royal, the Royal Hotel, the Post Office and the Municipal Buildings were lost for ever. But the people of Plymouth were unbowed. Thousands left the city each night for the foothills of Dartmoor and safety from the bombs, and returned to work the next day. The shell of St Andrew's Church was planted with flowers and hundreds came to worship in the 'Garden Church', while on hot summer evenings,

THE PIER FROM BELOW *1889* 22375

thousands would come from the ruined city to dance on the Hoe with dignitaries like Lady Nancy Astor MP and cock a defiant snook at Nazism.

Once the war was over, thoughts turned to reconstruction. It is a local joke that what Hitler started, the town planners finished: it is true that the new, geometric street plan of the city centre is a little uninspiring, but St Andrew's still stands, and the broad sweep of Armada Way leads one seawards to the heights of the Hoe.

Stand on the Promenade on a clear day and turn through 360°, and all around are reminders of Plymouth's past. To the north are the blue hills of Dartmoor, source of the tin that caused the port to come into existence. West is the entrance to the Tamar, home to the frigates, aircraft carriers and submarines which slip in and out of port in all weathers, even in peacetime. Merchantmen anchor in the lee of the Breakwater, ready to discharge their cargoes of petrol and fertiliser on the wharves of the Plym, and trawlers set sail from a largely unchanged Barbican for the fishing grounds. And on the horizon, the Eddystone light winks unceasingly, a beacon for mariners heading for one of Britain's great ports.

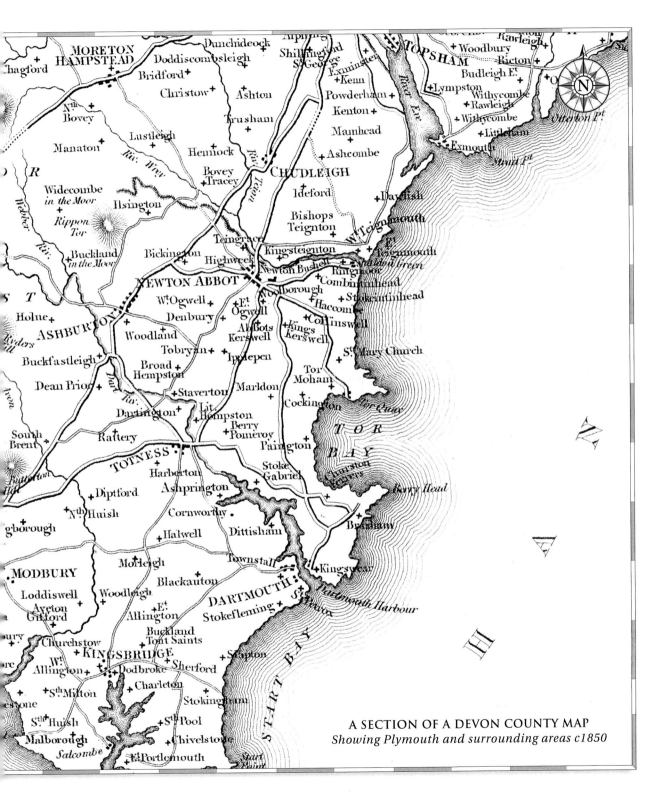

A SECTION OF A DEVON COUNTY MAP
Showing Plymouth and surrounding areas c1850

THE HOE AND THE BARBICAN

THE HOE *1890* 22471

Taken from Devil's Point looking across Firestone Bay with the Hoe just visible on the far right. The large colonnaded building is the Winter Villa, built by the Earl of Mount Edgecumbe for his wife, who found the winters at Mount Edgecumbe House a little too draughty.

VIEW FROM THE HOE *c1876* 8349

Taken from the site of the old Hoe Police Station and lock-up before the pier was built, this view shows a largely undeveloped West Hoe (the grassy area at centre). The large block of houses on the point at centre left still stands and is now mostly hotels.

THE HOE AND THE BARBICAN

THE ESPLANADE AND HOE *1889* 22363

One hundred feet above sea level, and with commanding views of the Sound and the English Channel, the Hoe is where Sir Francis Drake is reputed to have played his famous game of bowls while waiting for the Armada to arrive in 1588.

THE HOE AND PIER *1889* 22368

The prominent structure on the top of Staddon Heights (just right of centre) is not, as local myth says, a windbreak for the golf course on the top of the Heights; it was actually constructed as a gunnery range for troops stationed at Bovisand Fort, on the headland below.

THE ESPLANADE HOE *1889* 22361

The fine colonnaded building second from left is the Grand Hotel; it still stands, as does Eliot Terrace to its right. 3 Eliot Terrace was the home of Lord and Lady Astor for many years. Nancy Astor was the first woman MP in the country, representing Plymouth Sutton from 1919–46.

THE HOE AND THE BARBICAN

THE PIER FROM SMEATON'S TOWER
1889 22372

In the middle distance to the right are ships anchored in the Hamoaze, which turns north up the Tamar to Devonport Dockyard. The narrow entrance to the Hamoaze (hidden at centre) is easily guarded but, in times of sail, presented difficulties for the fleet if it needed to sail in a hurry and on a foul tide.

THE PIER FROM BELOW *1889 22375*

The building next to the Grand Hotel, a victim of the Luftwaffe in the blitz, became the home of the Royal Western Yacht Club in 1880. The club subsequently moved to West Hoe and, in the 1980s, to Queen Anne's Battery. The doors above the steps on the right were for many years used by the Leander Swimming Club.

SMEATON'S TOWER *1890* 22365

This lighthouse once occupied the feared Eddystone Rock, 14 miles south of the Hoe. Built by John Smeaton, it was the third lighthouse on the rock; it shone from 1756 to 1890, when the present lighthouse, designed by Douglas, was completed.

THE HOE AND THE BARBICAN

MOUNT EDGECUMBE
1889 22385

The wooded estate of Mount Edgecumbe is the hereditary seat of the Earls of Mount Edgecumbe. The clearing in the centre is the site of the famous folly, while on the right the top of Mount Edgecumbe House can be seen peeping from the trees.

THE PIER *1889* 22377

Plymouth's pier was destroyed in the blitz. It was built in 1884, extending out from the old Bull Ring, a popular spot for political meetings, particularly in the last century during the noisy campaign that led in 1832 to Plymouth becoming three constituencies and Stonehouse and Devonport having their own MPs for the first time.

THE HOE AND PIER
1890 27530

The centre of the pier, now covered, was a popular venue for concert parties, boxing, wrestling, roller skating and tea dances. To take the sea air in the company of other fashionable Victorians, one entered through the turnstiles on each side of the clock for the princely sum of 2d.

VIEW FROM THE PIER *1892* 30590

The building high up on the left houses the Plymouth Laboratory of the Marine Biological Association of Great Britain, now one of the world's leading marine research organisations. The building also housed the aquarium before the opening of the national marine aquarium on the Barbican in 1998. Right of the MBA is the Citadel, the city's biggest fortress.

THE HOE AND THE BARBICAN

Left: **THE PIER** *1892* 30585

The steps and diving board below the Sunlight Soap advertisement belonged to the Plymouth Ladies' Swimming Club. One ex-member recalls completing the two-mile swim from the Breakwater in 1927 in 58 minutes and two thirds of a second. Her sister held the record of 48 minutes.

Below: **VIEW FROM THE PIER** *1892* 30591

The rocks in the centre are where Tinside Pool now stands. Further back, to the right of the triangular buttress, is the site of the Royal Plymouth Corinthian Yacht Club and beyond that, the Cattewater.

THE PIER AND DRAKE'S ISLAND *1892*
30583

Drake's Island was originally known as St Nicholas Island; it was owned by the Priors of Plympton, who used it as a rabbit warren. It was fortified in 1549 and the defences were later extended by Plymouth's favourite son - hence the name change.

VIEW FROM STADDON *1889* 22383

The Mountbatten peninsula (foreground) guards and shelters the Cattewater and Sutton Pool (right). Occupied since prehistoric times, ownership was returned to the city in 1995 after nearly 70 years of occupation by the RAF. In the 1920s the personnel list included one Aircraftman Shaw - Lawrence of Arabia.

THE PIER *1898* 41930

The five square miles of Plymouth Sound provide a fine safe anchorage. Jennycliff Bay (in the middle distance on the left) is as popular a spot now as in 1898, especially if the wind is in the east and the great bulk of Staddon Heights acts as a natural windbreak.

THE HOE AND THE BARBICAN

**VIEW FROM
SMEATON POINT**
1898 41929

The curious octagonal building in the foreground was once the Hoe Police Station and was also a camera obscura. The building by the little harbour was for many years the home of the Royal Western Yacht Club and is now the Waterfront Restaurant.

THE BREAKWATER *1893* 31954

The completion of the Breakwater in 1844 after 32 years' work secured Plymouth's standing as a major port. Designed by John Rennie, and utilising 3,500,000 tons of limestone from quarries at Oreston, its construction meant that for the first time ships did not have to use the Plym or the Tamar to anchor in a storm.

THE HOE AND THE BARBICAN

THE HOE *1902* 48781

The bandstand (foreground) once stood on the site of today's public bowling green before moving to this site near Smeaton's Tower. Regular performers included the Royal Marine Band; the bandstand was hit during the blitz and subsequently pulled down.

THE PIER *1898* 41931

The paddle steamers ran trips to the River Yealm and as far west as Looe. In a curious echo of history, many of today's tourist boats leave from the site of the old pier for similar destinations, and also for cruises up the Tamar.

THE HOE *1904* 52403

The area covered by trees below the octagonal Police Station was for a long time home to the Mallard Café; it is now the site of the Dome, one of Plymouth's major attractions.

THE HOE AND THE BARBICAN

THE HOE *1904* 52398

The prominent building in the centre was used for many years as a nursery by the city parks department. The exposed position of the bandstand meant that it had to have a revolving glass screen to prevent the performers' music blowing away!

THE BANDSTAND *1902* 48782

In the middle distance on the left are the masts of ships in the lee of Drake's Island. Behind the row of terraced houses in the middle distance lie the Millbay Docks which were busy during the 1920s with passengers being ferried from the railway out to liners such as the 'Queen Mary' and 'Normandie'.

THE HOE AND THE BARBICAN

THE PIER *1913* 65981

Modern excursion boats are diesel rather than steam, and have propellers instead of paddle wheels. Paddlers lasted longer than is generally known, however: the dockyard was using paddle tugs until the mid 1980s.

THE HOE, *Smeaton's Tower and the Bandstand 1913* 65980

The stone pavilion on the left, known to Plymothians as the 'Wedding Cake', was built in 1891-2 when Alderman Harris was mayor. The garden directly below it is now a garden of remembrance to the dead of Dunkirk, Normandy, Korea, Malaysia and other campaigns.

SMEATON'S TOWER AND THE BANDSTAND *1913* 65979

As well as being used for promenading, the Hoe has always been the vantage point from which Plymothians have watched the arrivals and departures of vessels, from Sir Francis Chichester's 'Gypsy Moth IV' to the battle-weary ships of the Falklands war. In the 21st century, the Hoe and all the hills around Plymouth were lined with thousands of people welcoming home Dame Ellen MacArthur, who on February 7 2005 broke the world record for the fastest solo circumnavigation of the globe.

THE HOE AND THE BARBICAN

THE PIER *1924* 75896

The pier not only acted as a magnet for tourists but also for local traders, who would set up their carts, wagons and stalls near the entrance hoping to catch some trade from alighting tram passengers.

THE HOE AND THE BARBICAN

THE PIER AND DRAKE'S ISLAND *1924* 75899

On his return from his circumnavigation in 1580, Francis Drake anchored in the lee of the island while he sent messengers ashore to check if Queen Elizabeth was still alive and, if so, whether he was still in favour. He managed to ensure the latter by sending several tons of stolen Spanish gold to London.

THE NAVAL AND ARMADA MEMORIALS *1924* 75908

In 1888 the Hoe became a park and the Armada Memorial (left) was erected to mark the tercentenary of Drake's great victory. The Naval Memorial was extended considerably after the Second World War.

THE HOE AND THE BARBICAN

THE LIDO AND WALKS
1934 86216

The magnificent art deco Tinside Lido and Swimming Pool, completed in 1933, was a popular venue for generations of Plymouth children, mainly during the summer holidays, as the salt-water pool had no heating. More sedentary pleasures could be had by hiring a chalet, the roofs of some of which can be seen in the left foreground.

DRAKE'S STATUE *1930* 83293

The Café on the left was one of Hitler's victims; it was replaced by a vast Nissen Hut, which served teas well into the 1980s. Visible just behind Drake's Statue is the corner of the bowling green. The terrace behind is also gone; the Register Office now stands on the site.

THE ROYAL CITADEL GATE *1924* 75921

Construction of the Citadel commenced in 1670 on the orders of Charles II. It is now home to 29 Commando Regiment Royal Artillery; it was considerably extended in the 1980s. Just visible through the gate are some of the magnificent Restoration buildings that surround the parade ground.

Left: **FROM THE CITADEL** *1904*
52400

On the far right of the photograph, the building with the conservatory and tower is the old Hoegate School. The fine avenue of elm trees on the left suffered greatly from the ravages of Dutch Elm Disease in the 1970s.

Right: **THE SOUTH AFRICAN MEMORIAL** *1904* 52404

Only a year old when this photograph was taken, this pink granite obelisk was erected in memory of Christian Victor, Prince of Schleswig Holstein and grandson of Queen Victoria, who died in the Boer War. It also serves as a memorial to the men of the Gloucestershire, Somerset and Devonshire Regiments who died in the same campaign. A chip on the south-west corner is shrapnel damage from the blitz.

THE HOE AND THE BARBICAN

THE SOUTH AFRICAN MONUMENT AND GUILDHALL *1904* 52399

This view shows the commanding field of fire available to gunners on the Citadel, from where this picture was taken. Plymouth was staunchly parliamentarian during the Civil War; when Charles II built the Citadel, the fact that there were gun emplacements facing inland would not have gone unnoticed by the local population.

THE BARBICAN *1890* 22474

Built around Sutton Pool, site of one of the original settlements in the area, the Barbican is home to Plymouth's fishing fleet. The cobbled streets and granite steps remain unchanged, but in place of shipping offices and fish salesmen are now ice cream parlours, cafés and souvenir shops.

THE HOE AND THE BARBICAN

SUTTON POOL *1904*
52413A

*Declining stocks and fish
quotas have taken their toll
of the fleet, and Sutton Pool
now has far fewer boats. The
building on the right is the old
Barbican Police Station, now
used for other purposes, and
the quay has been extended
slightly so that the mooring
bollards now sprout from the
pavement!*

ONION SELLERS *1907* 59208

*The onions on the shoulders of these two boys, photographed at the Mayflower Steps, may well have been French. Breton
onion sellers were once a common sight on the streets of Plymouth.*

THE HOE AND THE BARBICAN

THE BARBICAN *c1955*
P60050

The open building on the left, now occupied by Dartington Glass, was until the 1990s the old fish market, built in 1892. The warehouses in the background have been converted into flats, and the area of Sutton Pool on the far right is now a marina.

THE BARBICAN *c1955* P60069

The white painted steps, centre left, are the Mayflower Steps, scene of the Pilgrim Fathers' departure for the New World in 1620. On the right, the coal wharf is now home to the new fish market and National Marine Aquarium, and the harbour now has lock gates to prevent it drying out at low tide.

'Janners' is a term used for people born in Plymouth; it is a less formal term than Plymothians. A 'janner' originally described a person who lived within sight of the sea, but is now used more generally for inhabitants of the whole city.

Plymouth's historical isolation was eased in 1758 with the completion of the Great West Road, but it still took twelve hours to reach Exeter!

Can you answer this old riddle?
Woman on a wheel,
Ship on the sea,
Eddystone Lighthouse,
What can it be?

ONE PENNY PIECE
showing the Eddystone Lighthouse 1948 F6050

The answer is: an old-fashioned penny. All these symbols were on the obverse. The woman on a ship's wheel was Britannia, ruling the waves, with the Eddystone lighthouse to the left and a ship to the right. In 1859 the Royal Mint commissioned Leonard Charles Wyon to design new coinage with a new portrait of Queen Victoria, and the farthing, halfpenny and one penny coins featured the Eddystone Lighthouse to commemorate the centenary of its building by John Smeaton. A new design, showing the 1882 Eddystone lighthouse but omitting the ship to the right of Britannia, was introduced in 1937 on one penny coins, and this remained on the penny until decimilisation in 1971.

Francis Drake began his historic circumnavigation of the world in the 'Golden Hind' from Plymouth in 1577; no other ship had ever made such a voyage before. When he returned to England in 1580 he was knighted by Elizabeth I. In 1966-67 Francis Chichester became the first man to sail single-handed around the world. He was knighted by Elizabeth II, using the same sword as that used by her predecessor for knighting Drake.

Prince Maurice Road and Mount Gould are named after the Royalist and Parliamentarian commanders of the Civil War forces which fought at Plymouth in 1643, Prince Maurice and Colonel Gould.

The oldest surviving domestic building in Plymouth is Prysten House, close to St Andrew's Church, in Finewell Street. It was built by Thomas Yogge in 1498, and is a fine limestone building with a galleried courtyard. The bottom floor of the house is let out as a restaurant, Tanners. In the past the building has been used as a dwelling house, a warehouse, a wine store and a bacon factory, but has belonged to St Andrew's Church since the 1920s and is used with the adjoining Abbey Hall for community purposes, and as a working museum. A model of Plymouth as it was in 1620 can be seen, and of interest is the 28ft Plymouth Tapestry, which depicts the colonisation of America. This took four and a half years to complete, and is made up of 2,250,000 stitches, some of which were added by royalty.

The Devon city of Plymouth has given its name to some 40 other Plymouths around the English-speaking world. The Pilgrim Fathers put in to Plymouth for repairs and provisions in 1620 before sailing to the New World, the final point of departure from mainland Britain of the 'Mayflower', eventually to land near that part of America still known as Plymouth Rock.

FROM THE AIR

PLYMOUTH *from the air 1937*   AF54888

FASCINATING FACTS

Several memorable voyages of exploration and discovery began from Plymouth; for example, Captain Cook left from Plymouth in 1768 on his voyage to chart New Zealand, and Charles Darwin sailed from here aboard the 'Beagle' in 1831. The observations that Darwin made on his voyage inspired his revolutionary theory about evolution, published as 'The Origin of Species', which questioned the account of the creation of the world in the Bible. A plaque on the Barbican also commemorates the departure from Plymouth in May 1839 of the 'Tory', the pioneer ship in the colonisation of New Zealand.

One of Devon's most famous sons was the former Royal Naval captain, Robert Falcon Scott, 'Scott of the Antarctic.' He was born near Plymouth in 1868, and became a national hero when he set the new 'furthest south' record with his expedition to Antarctica on 'Discovery' in 1901-1904. He came within 410 miles of the South Pole on this expedition, and set out on a further attempt to be the first man to reach this point in 1910, on board the 'Terra Nova'. He and his team arrived in Antarctica on 11 January 1911, but ran into difficulties almost immediately when their mechanical sledges failed due to the cold, and their ponies had to be shot because they could not survive the weather. At the same time a second explorer, the Norwegian Amundsen, was also racing them to the South Pole; using dogs to pull his sledges, he made rapid progress and reached the Pole in December 1911. Scott's five-man team were unaware of this, and were running short of supplies. They reached the South Pole on 17 January 1912, only to find out the heartbreaking news that they had been beaten by the Norwegians. Their challenge now was to return safely to their base, but with the team suffering from starvation, hypothermia and other illnesses this was not to be. Petty Officer Evans was the first to die, and then Captain Oates walked out of the party's tent on his 32nd birthday in March 1912, after delivering one of the most famous parting lines in history: 'I am just going outside and may be some time.' He never came back. As a blizzard raged outside the tent the other three team members could only await the inevitable, yet they were only 11 miles away from a fuel and food depot. Before his death, Scott wrote in his diary: 'We shall stick it out till the end, but we are getting weaker, of course, and the end cannot be far. It seems a pity but I do not think I can write more.'

HMS 'Implacable', seen in photograph 22467 on page 76, had one of the most extraordinary careers of any ship to sail. Launched in France in 1793 as the 'Duguay Trouin', at Trafalgar in 1805 she engaged Nelson's flagship, HMS 'Victory', and was eventually captured a few days later by HMS 'Hero'. Refitted at Devonport and renamed the 'Implacable', she fought in many battles before eventually becoming part of the HMS 'Lion' training establishment. She was decommissioned in 1904 and was eventually scuttled off the Isle of Wight in 1949.

The Crownhill Fort, built in 1863, is known locally as Plymouth's best kept secret. This elaborate Victorian fort was the principal, and largest, fort of Plymouth's North-Eastern Defences, intended to defend the Royal Dockyard at Devonport from an attack by the French from the north. At the time of its construction Crownhill represented the cutting edge of fortress design and, because of its exposed position, was designed for all-round defence, making it unlike any other fort in the Plymouth defences. It has seven sides, each with massive ramparts, and is surrounded by a deep dry ditch; each flank of the fort was defended by gunfire from projecting caponiers. The anticipated threat from the French never materialised, and Crownhill and its guns were never put to the ultimate test. However, Crownhill was retained by the army for over a century and used by a succession of infantry regiments when the Fort was used as HQ Plymouth Garrison. It is believed that anti-aircraft guns were positioned inside the Fort during the Second World War, making it the only time that the Fort saw action. Its military use ended in 1983. In 1986 the Fort was sold to the Landmark Trust. It has now been restored and is open to visitors; the staff dress up in Victorian costumes and offer period outfits for younger visitors and there is a daily gun firing at 1.30pm, a reminder of Crownhill Fort's former role as part of Plymouth's mighty Victorian 'Ring of Fire'.

ST ANDREW'S CHURCH
1889 22399

St Andrew's is the mother church of Plymouth; there is evidence that a Christian community used the site as early as the 8th century. Construction of the present building commenced in 1370. The church was burned down in the blitz, but restoration started in 1949 and the church was finally reconsecrated in 1957.

ST ANDREW'S CROSS *1900* 45862

After St Andrew's had been reduced to a shell by the Luftwaffe in 1941, somebody put a wooden board above the door with the word Resurgam on it, from the Latin for 'I will rise again'. Ever since then the north door (left) of St Andrew's has been known as the Resurgam door.

THE CITY

THE GUILDHALL
1889 22394

The fine tower at the west end of St Andrew's, built by Thomas Yogge in 1481 and now housing a peal of ten bells, used to look out over Guildhall Square, which is now a car park.

THE GUILDHALL AND POST OFFICE *1889* 22388

The Guildhall (left) and Municipal Buildings (right, containing the Lord Mayor's Parlour) were opened in 1874 by the Prince of Wales, who later became Edward VII. They were both gutted by fire on the night of 3 March 1941.

ST ANDREW'S CROSS 1895 36320

Erected in 1895 as a memorial after the removal of an ancient burial ground, St Andrew's Cross was damaged the night before the church went up in flames and was subsequently removed. The only remaining piece is the copper cross from the very top, which is now in the north aisle of St Andrew's.

THE CITY

THE GUILDHALL
1889 22395

Taken from the vicinity of the Boer War memorial, this picture shows how much more ornate the Guildhall was before its destruction and subsequent rebuilding. The spire on the ridge of the main roof no longer exists, and the tower now has a plain copper roof.

THE GUILDHALL AND POST OFFICE *1904* 52408

The main public entrance to the Post Office is just out of sight around the corner on the right. Staff entered through the central doors. Telegraphy equipment was housed on the first floor, and the top floor contained the staff rest-rooms.

THE GUILDHALL
1924 75920

The new stained glass window in the tower of St Andrew's, installed after the war, was designed by John Piper (who also designed the windows in the east end); it commemorates Nancy Astor and her husband, who were Mayor and Mayoress of Plymouth during the war years.

OLD TOWN STREET *1889* 22398

The modern Old Town Street runs more or less on the path of the old one. The spot where the carriage is driving is now on the pavement to the west of the Roundabout at St Andrew's Cross and on the south side of Royal Parade.

THE CITY

BEDFORD STREET
1904 52407

*The imposing Prudential
Building (centre) was
damaged during the war, but
still stood in 1945. It was
demolished in 1947 to make
way for the new street plan.
Its tower occupied a position
which today is on the west
side of Armada Way near
where the 'Western Morning
News' office now stands.*

BEDFORD STREET *1913* 65976

*This scene shows some well-known Plymouth businesses. Dingles (far left)
are still in the town, although these days owned by House of Fraser, and
Underwoods were well-known grocers. John Yeo, along with Spooners (out of
sight at the end of the street) was eventually taken over by Debenhams.*

THE CITY

THE GUILDHALL AND BEDFORD STREET *1904*
52409

The Bedford Hotel later became Bateman's Opticians, with a giant pair of spectacles that many local people still remember. The northern end of the Post Office (just visible down Basket Street in the centre) would now be on Royal Parade outside Dingles.

BEDFORD STREET *1913* 65975

Here we see more well-known Plymouth names. Many Plymothians remember buying school bags and suitcases from Webb and Son, who dealt in leather goods. Goodbody's Café was a popular spot, and indeed there is still a pub of that name on Mutley Plain.

OLD TOWN STREET
c1960 P60085

After the war, the remains of the city centre were demolished to make way for a new, more regular street plan. In this picture the new Post Office is still under construction on the right.

ROYAL PARADE *c1960* P60101

This photograph was taken from roughly the site of the old Post Office. The bus on the other side of Royal Parade behind the scooter is one of the first to have the door at the front and no conductor.

THE CITY

Left: **DRAKE'S CIRCUS** *c1950* P60032

The Guinness clock at the top of Old Town Street was a popular rendezvous. It stood where the southern end of Drake's Circus shopping centre now stands. The corner this side of the obvious awnings is now home to Burton's.

Below: **COBOURG STREET** *c1940* P60038

The north side of Cobourg Street is almost unchanged. The Public Secondary School (right), whose most well-known old girl is Angela Rippon, is now part of the University of Plymouth, and the playground is occupied by satellite dishes.

POUND STREET
c1955 P60051

To the right of the junction at the far end of Pound Street in this photograph is the Harvest Home, a much-loved pub which was demolished in 1964. The tall building beyond the Harvest Home still stands.

THE MUSEUM AND FREE LIBRARY *1892* 30581A

Although bombed during the war, the museum, art gallery and library are still at the bottom of Tavistock Road. Just out of the picture on the left was the surgery of the school dentist - something pointed out by almost every Plymothian over the age of 50 who sees this picture!

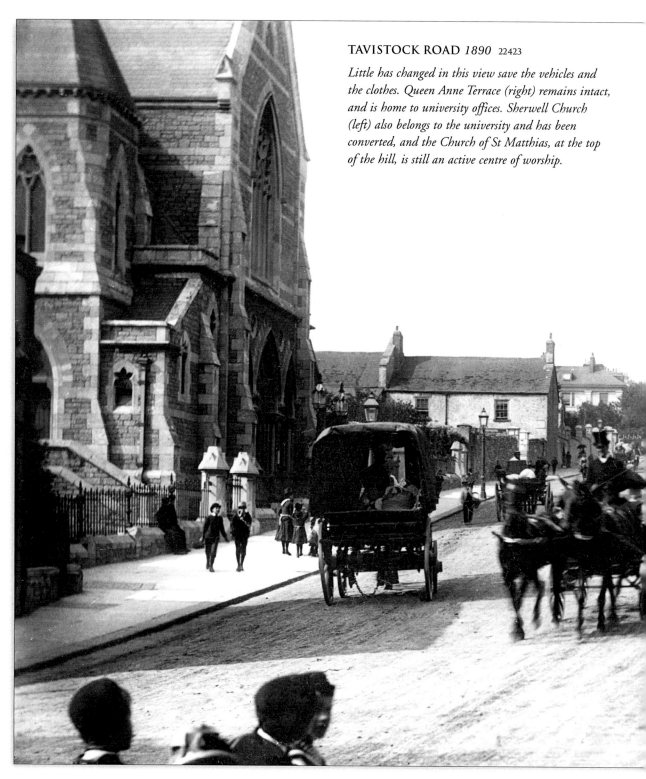

TAVISTOCK ROAD *1890* 22423

Little has changed in this view save the vehicles and the clothes. Queen Anne Terrace (right) remains intact, and is home to university offices. Sherwell Church (left) also belongs to the university and has been converted, and the Church of St Matthias, at the top of the hill, is still an active centre of worship.

MUTLEY PLAIN
1904 52412

The private houses on the left are now occupied by pizza take-aways and newsagents. The Co-op is still on the same premises, albeit with a new frontage, and Mutley Baptist Church (left) remains unchanged. The house on the corner of Alexandra Road (right) was for many years a dentist's.

MUTLEY PLAIN *1904* 52413

Take away the trees, update the shop frontages and turn the road into a dual carriageway, and you see Mutley as it is today, except that the Hyde Park Hotel (from where this view was taken) is now on an island and Mutley Methodist Church (left) has been pulled down.

Right: **THE CATHOLIC CATHEDRAL** *1889* 22409

The Cathedral Church of St Margaret Mary, with its elegant slim spire, was started in 1856 by Bishop Vaughan. Next to it in this picture stands Notre Dame High School, run by nuns who lived in the convent attached to the school. The site is now occupied by sheltered housing.

Below: **GEORGE STREET** *1889* 22397

The imposing columns are the entrance to the Theatre Royal, which stood on the site now occupied by the ABC Cinema. Theatregoers used to be able to hire a boy from the Barbican to queue for them, a service which cost the princely sum of 6d in the 1930s.

THE CLOCK TOWER *1892* 30597

Cousins' Hotel (left) and Genoni's, next to it, were popular refreshment stops for actors and stage crew between rehearsals. That function for the modern Theatre Royal (built roughly on the site of the GWR offices) is fulfilled by The Bank, which in this picture (behind the columns) is still a bank.

THE THEATRE ROYAL AND DERRY'S CLOCK *1907* 59204

Derry's Clock was erected in 1862 by William Derry during his second mayoralty to commemorate the marriage of the Prince of Wales (later Edward VII) and the Danish Princess Alexandra. It was known to generations of Plymothians as 'the four-faced deceiver' because all the clock faces told slightly different times. The clock still stands behind the new Theatre Royal.

THE CLOCK TOWER
1924 75922

Derry's Clock had four drinking fountains at its base with cups (long since gone) that hung on chains. The underground toilets on the right reputedly had their 'Ladies' and 'Gents' signs swapped round by Lawrence of Arabia when he was stationed in Plymouth under the assumed name of Aircraftman Shaw.

UNION STREET *1889* 22359

A surprising amount of this part of Union Street still exists. The corner on the left is now taxi offices and the adjoining buildings are night clubs and shops. The projecting building at centre left is the Clipper pub. The Octagon (centre) was in 1890 private homes rather than burger, pizza and kebab houses as now.

UNION STREET *1904* 52406

This view, taken in the direction of Stonehouse, shows some high street names that are still in business in the city today. Local lore has it that respectable ladies stuck to one side of the street, 'working girls' to the other, to avoid confusion.

DEVON RECIPES

'Great Drake, whose shippe aboute the world's wide wast
In three years did a golden girdle cast.
Who with fresh streames refresht this Towne that first
Though kist with waters, yet did pire for thirst.'

Up North Hill, on the left just after Sherwell church, is Drake's Reservoir. The reservoir itself was built in 1849 on Drake's Leat, Plymouth's original water supply, which was built by Sir Francis Drake in 1590-91 at a cost of £300. The leat brought water seventeen miles from the head of the River Meavy, 'carried every way to get the vantage of the hills'. The distance as the crow flies is only nine miles, and the leat represents a fair engineering achievement. It not only supplied clean water to Plymouth, but also powered several mills. For the last 400 years, the bringing of fresh water to Plymouth by Drake has been celebrated by the annual 'Fyshinge Feaste' in June. The Mayor of Plymouth and his council congregate at the head weir of the leat, where official toasts are drunk, from a goblet filled with water from the leat, 'to the pious memory of Sir Francis Drake'. Another goblet, this time filled with red wine, is then passed round, with each person drinking a further toast: 'May the descendants of him who brought us water never want'. As part of the tradition, a meal of local trout caught from the leat is eaten.

TROUT WITH ALMONDS AND CREAM

4 trout, gutted and cleaned
Flour for coating the fish
Salt and pepper
175g/6oz butter
50g/2oz blanched almonds
Juice of half a lemon
150ml/¼ pint single cream

Mix the flour with salt and pepper and use to coat the fish on both sides. Melt 100g/4oz of the butter in a frying pan. Slide in the trout and cook for 15 minutes, turning halfway through cooking time, until they are golden brown on both sides and cooked through. Drain the trout and keep warm on a serving dish.

Clean the pan, then melt the remaining butter in it. Add the almonds and fry carefully until they are lightly browned. Stir in the lemon juice. Heat the cream gently in a separate pan and pour over the fish. Sprinkle with the almonds and serve.

Sir Walter Raleigh is famous for introducing the ordinary potato to England from the New World, but Plymouth's Sir Francis Drake and Sir John Hawkins brought sweet potatoes to England in about 1563-65. Drake said of sweet potatoes: 'These potatoes be the most delicate rootes that may be eaten, and doe farre exceed out passeneps or carets. Their pines be of the bignes of two fists, the outside whereof is of the making of a pine-apple, but it is soft like the rinde of a cucomber, and the inside eateth like an apple but it is more delicious than any sweet apple sugared.' Sweet potatoes are now easily available in most supermarkets and greengrocer shops, and can be served in all the ways that ordinary potatoes are used, but cook much more quickly.

DEVON CIDER CAKE

250g/8oz mixed sultanas, raisins and currants
4 tablespoons sweet Devonshire cider
175g/6oz butter or margarine
175g/6oz soft brown sugar
3 eggs
250g/8oz self raising flour
1 teaspoon mixed spice (optional)

Soak the mixed fruits in the cider overnight. Cream the butter or margarine and add the sugar. Cream until fluffy. Lightly beat the eggs and gradually beat them into the mixture. Mix in the fruit and cider. Sift the flour and spice together, fold in half the flour, and mix well. Mix in the rest of the flour. Grease a 20cm/8 inch round or 18cm/7 inch square tin and line the bottom with greased, greaseproof paper. Bake in a moderate oven, 180 degrees C/350 degrees F/Gas Mark 4, for 1 hour and 10 minutes.

DEVONSHIRE FLATS

225g/8oz self raising flour
110/4oz caster sugar
100ml/3½fl oz Devonshire clotted or double cream
1 beaten egg
1 tablespoonful milk

Preheat the oven to 190 degrees C/375 degrees F/Gas Mark 5. Mix the flour and sugar together. Stir in the cream, egg and mix thoroughly with enough milk to make a stiff dough. Roll out the dough very thinly and cut into rounds of about 8cm/3 ins in diameter. Sprinkle with a little sugar and bake for about ten minutes, until lightly risen and golden brown.

DEVONSHIRE SQUAB PIE

675g/1½ lb lamb neck fillets, cut into 12 pieces
1 onion, thinly sliced
350g/12oz leeks, sliced
1 large cooking apple, peeled, cored and diced
Half a teaspoonful allspice
Half a teaspoonful freshly grated nutmeg
150ml/¼ pint lamb, beef or vegetable stock
225g/8oz shortcrust pastry
Beaten egg or milk, to glaze
Salt and pepper

Pre-heat the oven to 200 degrees C/400 degrees F/Gas Mark 6. Layer the meat, onion, leek and apple in a pie dish, sprinkling in the spices and seasoning as you go, to taste. Pour in the stock.

Roll out the pastry to 2cm/¾ inch larger than the top of the pie dish. Cut a narrow strip from around the pastry, fit it around the dampened rim of the dish, then brush with water. Lay the pastry over the dish, and press the edges together to seal them. Brush the pastry lid with beaten egg or milk, and make a hole in the centre.

Bake the pie in the pre-heated oven for 20 minutes, then reduce the oven temperature to 180 degrees C/350 degrees F/Gas Mark 4 and continue to cook for 1-1¼ hours, covering the pie with foil if the pastry begins to brown too much.

DEVONSHIRE SPLITS

These yeasted buns are served split open and filled with Devonshire clotted cream and jam. If served with clotted cream and black treacle, they are known as 'Thunder and Lightning'.

15g/½oz fresh yeast, or 10g/¼oz dried yeast
Half a teaspoon of caster sugar
150ml/¼ pint tepid water
75g/3oz butter or margarine
6 tablespoonfuls milk
450g/1lb plain flour
Pinch of salt
Icing sugar
Clotted cream and strawberry or raspberry jam to serve

Sprinkle the yeast and sugar over the tepid water and leave in a warm place until it is frothy. Put the butter or margarine and milk into a small saucepan and heat gently until the fat has melted - do not allow to boil. Remove from heat and allow to cool.

Sift the flour and salt into a mixing bowl, make a well in the centre and pour in the yeast and milk mixtures, then mix the dough until it is soft but not sticky. Turn on to a floured surface and knead gently for 5 minutes, then put into a bowl and leave covered in a warm place for 1 hour.

Take out and knead again a little, then shape into about 18 small balls. Place them on a greased baking sheet a little apart, and leave until they have spread and are just touching.

Bake in a pre-heated oven (200 degrees C/400 degrees F/Gas mark 6) for about 20 minutes, or until well risen. When cooked, they should sound hollow when tapped. Dust with icing sugar, and serve spilt open, spread with clotted cream and jam.

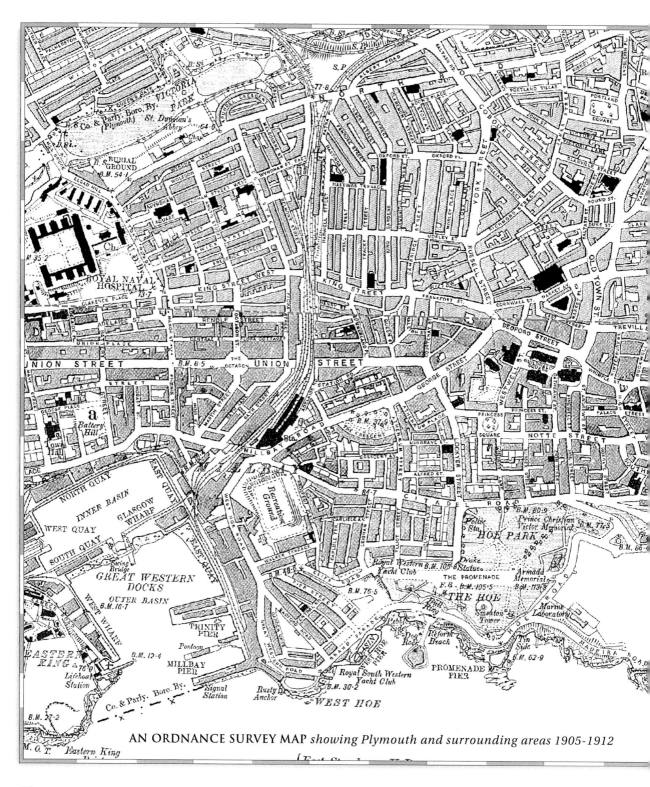

AN ORDNANCE SURVEY MAP *showing Plymouth and surrounding areas 1905-1912*

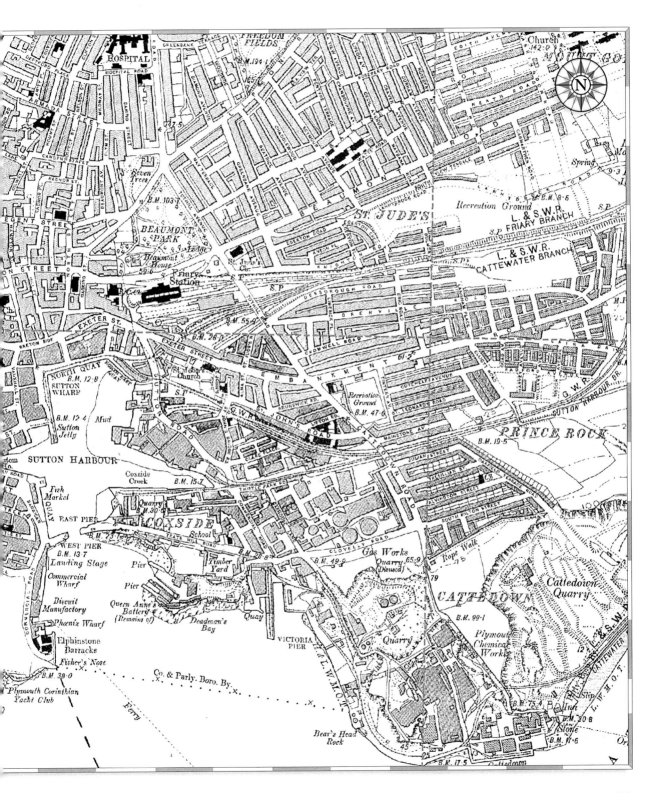

DEVONPORT AND THE RIVER TAMAR

DEVONPORT, *Halfpenny Bridge 1904* 52427

Upstream of Halfpenny Bridge, Stonehouse creek used to run as far as Pennycomequick, but was progressively filled over the years. Downstream (right) from the bridge is the Cremyll Ferry and Royal Willam Yard. The tollhouse was the white building on the left; the toll, as the name suggested, was a halfpenny.

DEVONPORT
Royal Marine Barracks 1890 22448

Situated on Durnford Street, which runs parallel to Stonehouse Creek, the Royal Marine Barracks were built in 1867 using a mixture of Plymouth limestone and granite from the moors and originally housed 1,400 men.

DEVONPORT, *Mount Wise 1890* 22468

A large marina now stands (or rather floats) on this site. The hill on the right has a memorial to Devonport's most famous son, Captain Scott (see page 46), and on the riverside in the middle distance the large barn-like building is King Billy Yard, the oldest covered shipyard still standing in Europe.

DEVONPORT
The Boer Gun 1904 52415A

Inscribed 'Ready Aye Ready', this captured Boer gun is a memorial to Royal Marines and sailors from HMS 'Doris'. Fittingly, it stands high on a hill overlooking the dockyard from which HMS 'Doris' would have sailed to South Africa.

DEVONPORT, *HMS 'Lion' and 'Implacable' 1890* 22467

These old ships of the line were probably used as training ships for young recruits. Outdated, mothballed or paid-off vessels were often moored at this spot off the mouth of Millbrook Lake. The much-loved aircraft carrier 'Ark Royal' spent some years here prior to being towed away for scrap in 1979.

DEVONPORT, *Torpoint Ferry Bridge 1890* 22462

Ferries crossed at this point since the 18th century, carrying not only people, carriages and goods but, from 1800, the post for the Truro coach. 'Jemima', built at Stonehouse, became the first steam ferry in service in 1826, but was quickly replaced by steam driven chain ferries.

TORPOINT, *The Ferry 1925* 78415

The earliest ferries were little more than two hulls with a platform suspended between them, and the crossing could take some time owing to the strong tides that run in the Tamar. Modern chain ferries, little affected by the tides, rattle and clank their way across in about ten minutes.

TORPOINT, *The Ferry c1955* T63003

The lorry at the head of the ferry queue is probably taking empties back to the Plymouth Brewery near Halfpenny Bridge in Stonehouse. Fondly remembered by older drinkers, Plymouth Brewery was eventually taken over by Courage; after that, the beer never tasted quite the same.

TORPOINT
The Ferry c1955 T63004

The steep loading ramp of the ferries caused problems for longer vehicles, which were in danger of grounding. The brown and cream Co-op coaches had a bevel taken off the rear bodywork to prevent this happening.

TORPOINT, *The Ferry c1955* T63006

At one time cars were fitted so tightly onto the ferries that it was impossible to open the doors. The obvious dangers of this in case of fire or sinking caused a public outcry, and eventually the ferries were widened.

TORPOINT
Fore Street c1955 T63014

On the left is Wheeler's Hotel, and at the top of the street, just visible, is the hop leaf symbol of Simond's Brewery - once a common sight on local pubs. On the right are two trade names that are rarely seen today - Woodbines and Capstan Full Strength.

TORPOINT, *Fore Street and the Ferry Queue c1955* T63015

The ferry queue no longer blocks Fore Street - it takes the road on the right down to a large waiting area by the river. The three men in white hats are probably 'Tiffies' - Artificers from the training establishment at HMS 'Fisgard', now closed.

DEVONPORT AND THE RIVER TAMAR

SALTASH, *The Royal Albert Bridge 1890* 22477

The rich fields of the Tamar Valley have long been the source of Plymouth's fruit and vegetables. Tamar barges such as the one in the centre of this picture would bring produce down from Calstock, Gunnislake and Bere Alston and land them at Cornwall Street in Devonport.

SALTASH, *The Royal Albert Bridge 1890* 22480

The Royal Albert Bridge, completed in 1859, is a fitting memorial to the great Victorian engineer Isambard Kingdom Brunel. The Admiralty stipulated that it must be at least 100ft above the water to allow the passage of ships.

PLYMPTON
St Mary's 1890 22512

On the right of the photograph in front of the church is the old priory. The monks had their own path through the woods to the church, where they had their own pews. Behind the church, hidden in the trees, is Plympton station, which closed in 1959, and in the centre of the picture is the old St Mary's Church of England School.

PLYMPTON, *The Town Hall 1890* 22515

This view remains almost unchanged, save that the horse and cart have been replaced by the motor car. The arched walk under the Town Hall is known as the Butterwalk.

PLYMPTON, *Ridgeway 1898* 41943

Matthews' Bun Shop (right) was so famous for its hot cross buns that people would walk for miles, even from Plymouth, to sample its wares. There were often long queues at 4.00am!

OUTLYING AREAS

FERRY HOUSE AND PLANTATIONS
1901 46333

The quiet estuary of the River Yealm (pronounced 'Yam') lies to the east of Plymouth. The foot ferry still runs at this spot, summoned by shouting 'over' or by whistling. The villages of Newton Ferrers and Noss Mayo lie just up the river to the left.

BERE FERRERS *1898* 42257

Bere Ferrers lies north of Plymouth on the isolated peninsula that divides the estuaries of the Tamar and its tributary the Tavy (right). Bere Ferrers is the first stop on the Tamar Valley railway line which runs up to Gunnislake; it has the distinction of being one of the few lines on which the train sometimes stops to allow passengers to take photographs!

84

DRAKE'S ISLAND
1890 22426

Now in Cornwall, Mount Edgecumbe, from where this picture was taken, was once part of Devon. The nearby village of Kingsand still has a stone showing where the boundary used to lie. The folly was constructed using stone from the tower of St Lawrence's Church, which used to stand on the site now occupied by Royal William Yard in Stonehouse.

DRAKE'S ISLAND FROM MOUNT EDGECUMBE *1890* 22427

The broad channel between Drake's Island and Mount Edgecumbe, known as The Bridges, is only navigable via one narrow channel, which is why ships always appear to take 'the long way round', following Drake Passage to the east and north of the Island, as the three-master in this picture is probably doing.

OUTLYING AREAS

PLYMOUTH
From Mount Edgecumbe 1890 22425

In the centre is the Edgecumbes' Winter Villa, which later became the convent and nursing home Nazareth House. It was completely rebuilt after a fire. The grassy area to the left is Devil's Point, a popular picnic and walking spot.

MOUNT EDGECUMBE HOUSE *1890* 22436

The building of Mount Edgecumbe House was started by Piers Edgecumbe in 1539 and remodelled in the 17th and 18th centuries. It was badly damaged by German incendiaries in March 1941 and subsequently restored, but the highest tower in this picture was never rebuilt.

INDEX

The Francis Frith Collection Titles

www.francisfrith.com

The Francis Frith Collection publishes over 100 new titles each year. A selection of those currently available is listed below. For latest catalogue please contact The Francis Frith Collection.

Town Books 96 pages, approximately 75 photos. **County and Themed Books** 128 pages, approximately 135 photos (unless specified).

Accrington Old and New
Alderley Edge and Wilmslow
Amersham, Chesham and Rickmansworth
Andover
Around Abergavenny
Around Alton
Aylesbury
Barnstaple
Bedford
Bedfordshire
Berkshire Living Memories
Berkshire Pocket Album
Blackpool Pocket Album
Bognor Regis
Bournemouth
Bradford
Bridgend
Bridport
Brighton and Hove
Bristol
Buckinghamshire
Calne Living Memories
Camberley Pocket Album
Canterbury Cathedral
Cardiff Old and New
Chatham and the Medway Towns
Chelmsford
Chepstow Then and Now
Cheshire
Cheshire Living Memories
Chester
Chesterfield
Chigwell
Christchurch
Churches of East Cornwall
Clevedon
Clitheroe
Corby Living Memories
Cornish Coast
Cornwall Living Memories
Cotswold Living Memories
Cotswold Pocket Album
Coulsdon, Chipstead and Woodmanstern
County Durham
Cromer, Sheringham and Holt
Dartmoor Pocket Album
Derby
Derbyshire
Derbyshire Living Memories
Devon

Devon Churches
Dorchester
Dorset Coast Pocket Album
Dorset Living Memories
Dorset Villages
Down the Dart
Down the Severn
Down the Thames
Dunmow, Thaxted and Finchingfield
Durham
East Anglia Pocket Album
East Devon
East Grinstead
Edinburgh
Ely and The Fens
Essex Pocket Album
Essex Second Selection
Essex: The London Boroughs
Exeter
Exmoor
Falmouth
Farnborough, Fleet and Aldershot
Folkestone
Frome
Furness and Cartmel Peninsulas
Glamorgan
Glasgow
Glastonbury
Gloucester
Gloucestershire
Greater Manchester
Guildford
Hailsham
Hampshire
Harrogate
Hastings and Bexhill
Haywards Heath Living Memories
Heads of the Valleys
Heart of Lancashire Pocket Album
Helston
Herefordshire
Horsham
Humberside Pocket Album
Huntingdon, St Neots and St Ives
Hythe, Romney Marsh and Ashford
Ilfracombe
Ipswich Pocket Album
Isle of Wight
Isle of Wight Living Memories
King's Lynn

Available from your local bookshop or from the publisher

See Frith books on the internet at www.francisfrith.com

FRITH PRODUCTS & SERVICES

Francis Frith would doubtless be pleased to know that the pioneering publishing venture he started in 1860 still continues today. Over a hundred and forty years later, The Francis Frith Collection continues in the same innovative tradition and is now one of the foremost publishers of vintage photographs in the world. Some of the current activities include:

Interior Decoration

Today Frith's photographs can be seen framed and as giant wall murals in thousands of pubs, restaurants, hotels, banks, retail stores and other public buildings throughout the country. In every case they enhance the unique local atmosphere of the places they depict and provide reminders of gentler days in an increasingly busy and frenetic world.

Product Promotions

Frith products are used by many major companies to promote the sales of their own products or to reinforce their own history and heritage. Frith promotions have been used by Hovis bread, Courage beers, Scots Porage Oats, Colman's mustard, Cadbury's foods, Mellow Birds coffee, Dunhill pipe tobacco, Guinness, and Bulmer's Cider.

Genealogy and Family History

As the interest in family history and roots grows world-wide, more and more people are turning to Frith's photographs of Great Britain for images of the towns, villages and streets where their ancestors lived; and, of course, photographs of the churches and chapels where their ancestors were christened, married and buried are an essential part of every genealogy tree and family album.

Frith Products

All Frith photographs are available Framed or just as Mounted Prints and Posters (size 23 x 16 inches). These may be ordered from the address below. From time to time other products - Address Books, Calendars, Table Mats, etc - are available.

The Internet

Already ninety thousand Frith photographs can be viewed and purchased on the internet through the Frith websites and a myriad of partner sites.

For more detailed information on Frith companies and products, look at this site:

www.francisfrith.com

See the complete list of Frith Books at:
www.francisfrith.com
This web site is regularly updated with the latest list of publications from The Francis Frith Collection. If you wish to buy books relating to another part of the country that your local bookshop does not stock, you may purchase on-line.

For further information, trade, or author enquiries please contact us at the address below:
The Francis Frith Collection, Frith's Barn, Teffont, Salisbury, Wiltshire, England SP3 5QP.
Tel: +44 (0)1722 716 376 Fax: +44 (0)1722 716 881 Email: sales@francisfrith.co.uk

See Frith books on the internet at www.francisfrith.com

FREE PRINT OF YOUR CHOICE

Mounted Print
Overall size 14 x 11 inches (355 x 280mm)

Choose any Frith photograph in this book.
Simply complete the Voucher opposite and
return it with your remittance for £3.50 (to cover
postage and handling) and we will print the
photograph of your choice in SEPIA (size 11 x 8
inches) and supply it in a cream mount with a
burgundy rule line (overall size 14 x 11 inches).
Please note: aerial photographs and
photographs with a reference number
starting with a "Z" are not Frith photographs
and cannot be supplied under this offer.
Offer valid for delivery to one UK address only.

PLUS: Order additional Mounted Prints
at HALF PRICE - £9.50 each (normally £19.00)
If you would like to order more Frith prints from
this book, possibly as gifts for friends and family,
you can buy them at half price (with no
additional postage and handling costs).

PLUS: Have your Mounted Prints framed
For an extra £18.00 per print you can have your
mounted print(s) framed in an elegant polished
wood and gilt moulding, overall size
16 x 13 inches (no additional postage and
handling required).

IMPORTANT!

**These special prices are only available if you use
this form to order. You must use the ORIGINAL
VOUCHER on this page (no copies permitted). We
can only despatch to one UK address. This offer
cannot be combined with any other offer.**

Send completed Voucher form to:
**The Francis Frith Collection, Frith's Barn,
Teffont, Salisbury, Wiltshire SP3 5QP**

CHOOSE A PHOTOGRAPH FROM THIS BOOK

Voucher for **FREE** and Reduced Price Frith Prints

*Please do not photocopy this voucher. Only the original is valid,
so please fill it in, cut it out and return it to us with your order.*

Picture ref no	Page no	Qty	Mounted @ £9.50	Framed + £18.00	Total Cost £
		1	Free of charge*	£	£
			£9.50	£	£
			£9.50	£	£
			£9.50	£	£
			£9.50	£	£
			£9.50	£	£

*Please allow 28 days
for delivery.
Offer available to one
UK address only*

* Post & handling £3.50

Total Order Cost £

Title of this book . . . .

I enclose a cheque/postal order for £ . . . .
made payable to 'The Francis Frith Collection'

OR please debit my Mastercard / Visa / Maestro card,
details below

Card Number

Issue No (Maestro only)   Valid from (Maestro)

Expires   Signature

Name Mr/Mrs/Ms . . . .
Address . . . .
. . . .
. . . .
. . . . Postcode . . . .
Daytime Tel No . . . .
Email . . . .

Valid to 31/12/12

Free Print – see overleaf

Can you help us with information about any of the Frith photographs in this book?

We are gradually compiling an historical record for each of the photographs in the Frith archive. It is always fascinating to find out the names of the people shown in the pictures, as well as insights into the shops, buildings and other features depicted.

If you recognize anyone in the photographs in this book, or if you have information not already included in the author's caption, do let us know. We would love to hear from you, and will try to publish it in future books or articles.

Our production team

Frith books are produced by a small dedicated team at offices in the converted Grade II listed 18th-century barn at Teffont near Salisbury, illustrated above. Most have worked with The Francis Frith Collection for many years. All have in common one quality: they have a passion for The Francis Frith Collection. The team is constantly expanding, but currently includes:

Andrew Alsop, Paul Baron, Jason Buck, John Buck, Jenny Coles, Heather Crisp, David Davies, Natalie Davis, Louis du Mont, Isobel Hall, Chris Hardwick, Neil Harvey, Julian Hight, Peter Horne, James Kinnear, Karen Kinnear, Tina Leary, Stuart Login, Sue Molloy, Sarah Roberts, Kate Rotondetto, Eliza Sackett, Terence Sackett, Sandra Sampson, Adrian Sanders, Sandra Sanger, Julia Skinner, Lewis Taylor, Will Tunnicliffe, David Turner and Ricky Williams.